TO THE TEACHER

In my many years of teaching piano to the young I **have** found that the theory of music, so necessary for good performance and musicianship, is best learned and **retained** through written work.

The lessons herewith have been used with excellent results and at the request of countless teachers met during my many workshops I am now making them available in printed form.

They are designed to supply written work that will make plainer than plain the facts in learning about music. Actually, theory is the language of music and to perform well one must speak and understand this "language" without hesitation.

The written work will not only train the student to observe carefully and to be accurate in what he does but will also serve as a help to the teacher in checking the student's comprehension of what he is learning.

The work progresses gradually and is planned to be suitable for use with any method or series of teaching materials either in class or private instruction.

It is suggested that these lessons be given the student one at a time.

EDNA MAE BURNAM

The music writing work in BOOK TWO is built on the following musical facts:

NOTES

KEY SIGNATURES

C Major	F Major
G Major	Bb Major
D Major	

TIME SIGNATURES

$\frac{2}{4}$ $\frac{3}{4}$ $\frac{4}{4}$ $\frac{5}{4}$ $\frac{6}{4}$

NOTE AND REST VALUES

MUSICAL SIGNS

tie	accent
slur	hold
triplet	staccato
D. C. al fine	repeat
D. S. al fine	sharp
First and second endings	flat
	natural
	"segno" sign

MUSICAL WORDS

Andante	Crescendo
Moderato	Diminuendo
Allegro	Accelerando
Legato	Forte
Fine	Mezzo forte
Tempo	Fortissimo
Da capo	Piano
Dal segno	Mezzo piano
Ritard	Pianissimo

W.M.Co., 9857

LESSON ONE

Pupil's Name _____ Date _____ Grade (or Star) _____

1. READING

Read this letter aloud.

Fill in the missing letters to see if you read the letter correctly.

WILL YOU —OM__ __N__ VISIT M__ THIS W __ __ K
__N__? W__ WILL G__ SWIMMIN__ __ND
H__V__ __UN. PL___S__ __NSW__R SOON. S__M.

2. WRITING

Write the name of the KEY SIGNATURE in the box under each of the following.

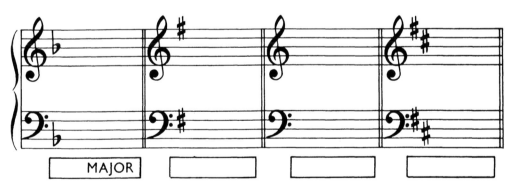

| MAJOR | | | |

3. COUNTING

Write in the note or rest needed in each line to make the correct count given at the end of the line.

♩ ♩ = 4		♩ = 4
♩ = 3		♪ = 2
♪ 𝄾 = 2		♩. = 4
𝄽 = 2		♩ = 2

4. SPELLING

Spell correctly as you write the abbreviation for each of the following:

Gradually louder _____

Gradually slower _____

Gradually softer _____

Gradually faster _____

HELPER

Word	Abbreviation	Meaning
Crescendo	Cresc.	Gradually louder
Diminuendo	Dim.	Gradually softer
Accelerando	Accel.	Gradually faster
Ritardando	Rit.	Gradually slower

5. DRAWING

Draw three more signs for gradually softer ====————

HELPER

This sign means gradually softer

======————

This sign means gradually louder

————======

Draw three more signs for gradually louder ————======

6. GAME

CROSS WORD PUZZLE

Print the correct words in the PUZZLE that the Cue List calls for.

Cue List

Down	Across	PUZZLE

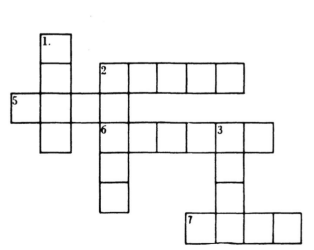

Down

↓

1. ⌢

2. (staff lines)

3. ♩

Across

→

2. ♯

5. ♭

6. >

7. 𝄾

BOOK TWO

LESSON TWO

Pupil's Name _____ Date _____ Grade (or Star) _____

1. READING

As you read the notes, print the letter names of them in the boxes above or below them.

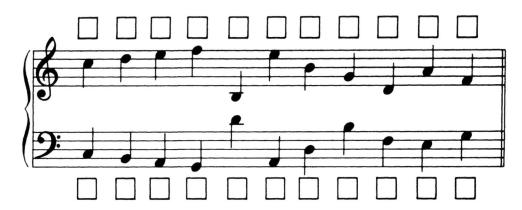

READ THIS ALOUD

2. WRITING

HELPER	
Word	**Meaning**
tempo	time (relating to speed)
allegro	lively, quickly
andante	slow, graceful
moderato	moderate speed
staccato	short, detached
legato	smoothly

Write the musical word to match each of the following:

lively, quickly _____

slow, graceful _____

moderate speed _____

smoothly _____

time (relating to speed) _____

short, detached _____

3. COUNTING

Count the number of beats and write the total in each box.

4. SPELLING

Spell the words that the notes represent. Print them in the boxes below.

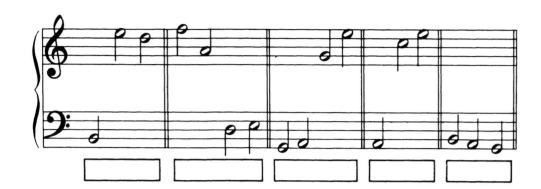

5. DRAWING

After each arrow, draw the musical signs for the following:

accent _____→

tie _____→

gradually louder _____→

hold _____→

staccato _____→

repeat _____→

gradually softer _____→

6. GAME

FIND THE OTHER HALF

Draw a line to the name of each Key Signature.

one sharp - F

two sharps - F, C

one flat - B

no sharps or flats

BOOK TWO

LESSON THREE

Pupil's Name _____ Date _____ Grade (or Star) _____

1. READING

READ THIS POEM ALOUD!

Fill in the missing letters to
see if you read the poem
correctly.

D __ WN __ T TH __ __ __ __ __ H N __ __ RLY __ V __ RYON __
RU __ S ON SUNT __ N LOTION,
TH __ N TH __ Y H __ V __ __ LOT O __ __ UN
RI __ IN __ W __ V __ S IN TH __ O __ __ __ N.

2. WRITING

Write the name of the KEY
SIGNATURE in the box under
each of the following.

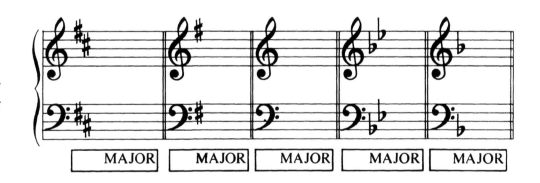

| MAJOR | MAJOR | MAJOR | MAJOR | MAJOR |

3. SPELLING

Write in the notes to spell
the words the notes represent
TWO TIMES. Once in the
treble and once in the bass
clef.

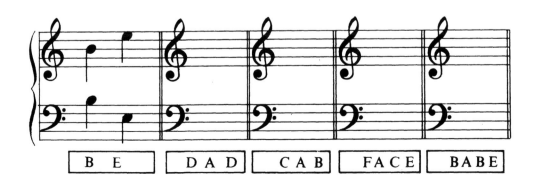

| B E | D A D | C A B | F A C E | B A B E |

W.M.Co., 9857

4. COUNTING

HELPER

Here are two new time signatures: In $\frac{5}{4}$ there are 5 beats to a measure. A quarter note receives one beat.

In $\frac{6}{4}$ there are 6 beats to a measure. A quarter note receives one beat.

Put in the bar lines and number the counts in each measure.

5. DRAWING

Draw the sign that means the same as the following:

Cresc.

Dim.

6. GAME

CROSS WORD PUZZLES.

Here are two Cross Word Puzzles. Print the correct abbreviations for words in the Puzzles that the Cue Lists call for.

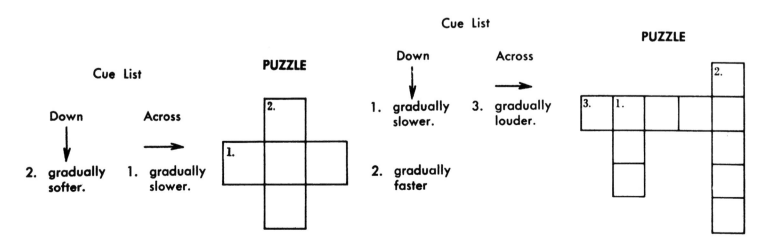

Cue List

Down
2. gradually softer.

Across
1. gradually slower.

PUZZLE

Cue List

Down
1. gradually slower.
2. gradually faster

Across
3. gradually louder.

PUZZLE

BOOK TWO
LESSON FOUR

Pupil's Name _____ Date _____ Grade (or Star) _____

1. READING

As you read the notes, print their letter names in the boxes above and below them.

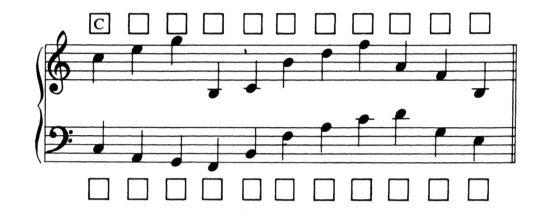

2. WRITING

Write the musical word to match each of the following:
HELPER — SEE LESSON TWO.

slow, graceful _____   moderate speed _____

lively, quickly _____   short, detached _____

3. COUNTING

Put in the time signatures and number the counts in each measure.

4. SPELLING

Spell the words that the notes represent. Print them in the boxes below.

W.M.Co., 9857

5. DRAWING

Draw a line from each musical word to the meaning for each word.

STACCATO

LEGATO

TEMPO

ANDANTE

MODERATO

ALLEGRO

smooth

slowly

moderate speed

quickly

short

time

6. GAME

CROSS WORD PUZZLE

USE WORDS IN NUMBER 5 FOR A "HELPER" IN DOING THIS PUZZLE.

Cue List

PUZZLE

Across

→

1. Short, detached.
2. Smoothly
3. Quickly, lively.
4. Moderate speed.

Down

↓

5. Slowly, graceful.
6. Time.

BOOK TWO
LESSON FIVE

Pupil's Name _____ Date _____ Grade (or Star) _____

1. READING Read this invitation aloud!
Watch the clef signs!!

YOU __ R __ INVIT __ __ TO __ P __ RTY

ON J __ NU __ RY __ IRST

__ T TWO O' __ LO __ K SH __ RP

IN TH __ Y. M. __ PL __ S __ OM

Fill in the missing letters to see if you read the invitation correctly.

YOU __ R __ INVIT __ __ TO __ P __ RTY
ON J __ NU __ RY __ IRST, __ T TWO O' __ LO __ K SH __ RP
IN TH __ Y. M. __. __. PL __ __ S __ __ OM __.

2. WRITING

As you read the letter names of these notes write them in the boxes above and below them.

3. COUNTING

Put a note or rest in each box to make the correct total for each of the following:

♩ ☐ ♩ ☐ = 5   ♫ ♪ ☐ = 4

♩ ♩ ☐ = 4   ♩ ♩ ♩ ☐ = 5

♩. ☐ ☐ = 6   ♩ ☐ ♩ ☐ = 6

♩ 𝄽 ☐ = 4   ♩ ☐ = 5

W.M.Co.. 9857

4. SPELLING

Spell words correctly as you complete these sentences:

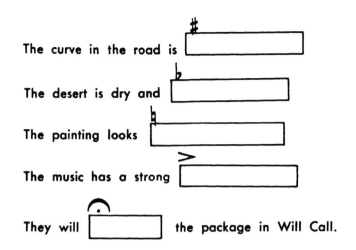

The curve in the road is _____

The desert is dry and _____

The painting looks _____

The music has a strong _____

They will _____ the package in Will Call.

5. DRAWING

Draw an arrow to each Key Signature and print the number of sharps or flats in it. Name the sharps or flats in correct order.

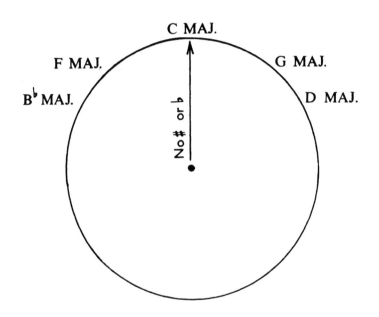

6. GAME
BINGO

Each square is numbered. Using the words below fill in each square correctly.

A BINGO may be vertical, horizontal or diagonal.

Find and cross off the winning BINGO and name the winner in the box below.

1 🎼	2	3	4	5
6	7	8	9	10
11	12	FREE	13	14
15	16	17	18	19
20	21	22	23	24

WINNER of BINGO

_____

1. Treble clef
2. Bass clef
3. Hold
4. Accent
5. Staccato
6. Quarter Note
7. Treble clef
8. Eighth note
9. Half note
10. Whole note
11. Eighth rest
12. Quarter rest
13. Repeat
14. Bass clef
15. Loud
16. Soft
17. Medium loud
18. Treble Clef
19. Very soft
20. Very loud
21. Two eighth notes
22. Dotted half note
23. Hold
24. Treble clef

BOOK TWO
LESSON SIX

Pupil's Name _____ Date _____ Grade (or Star) _____

1. READING

As you read the notes, print their names in the boxes above and below them.

2. WRITING

HELPER

A TIE is a curved line that joins two notes on the same line or space.

When two notes are tied, the second note is not struck — but is HELD for its full count.

A SLUR is a curved line that joins two or more notes that are NOT on the same line or space and these notes should be played smoothly.

Write "S" for Slur, or "T" for Tie in the boxes below.

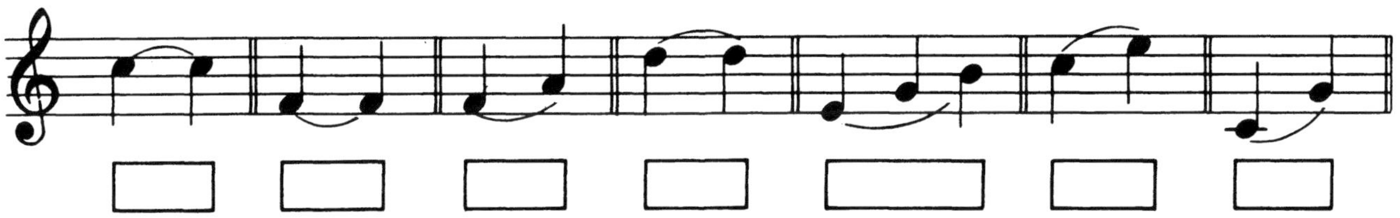

3. COUNTING

Put in the correct Time Signature for each of the following:

4. SPELLING

Spell the words that the notes represent. Print them in the boxes below.

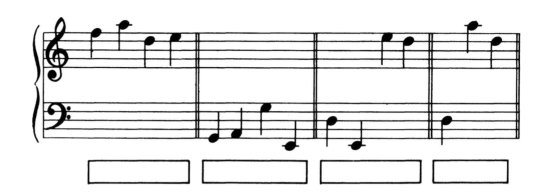

5. DRAWING

Draw a circle around every SLUR.

Draw a square around every TIE.

6. GAME
CATCH ME IF YOU CAN

Put a check mark like this X after the correct answer for each of the following:

smoothly .... { legato / staccato }

slow .... { moderato / andante / allegro }

gradually faster ..... { Cresc. / Dim. / Accel. / Rit. }

5/4 time signature ...

very loud .. { ff / pp }

key signature of D Major ..... { one flat / one sharp / two sharps / two flats / no sharps or flats }

slur ....

BOOK TWO

LESSON SEVEN

Pupil's Name _____ Date _____ Grade (or Star) _____

1. READING

As you read the notes, print their letter names in the boxes above and below them.

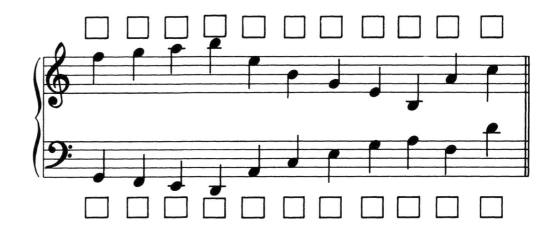

2. WRITING

Write the following as a MUSICAL ten word TELE-GRAM.

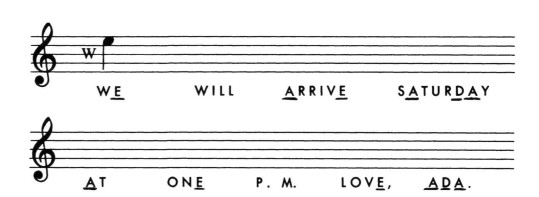

WE   WILL   ARRIVE   SATURDAY

AT   ONE   P. M.   LOVE,   ADA.

3. COUNTING

> **HELPER — TRIPLETS**
>
> A TRIPLET is a group of notes that receive one beat. The three notes of the TRIPLET have a curved line and the figure 3 over them, — like this —

Count the number of beats and write the total in each box.

16

4. SPELLING

Spell the words correctly as you fill in the boxes to complete these sentences.

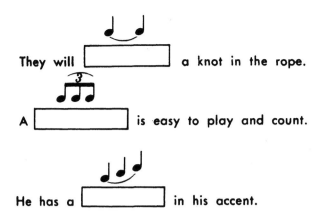

They will [   ] a knot in the rope.

A [   ] is easy to play and count.

He has a [   ] in his accent.

5. DRAWING

Draw the sign needed (SLUR, TIE or TRIPLET) for the following.

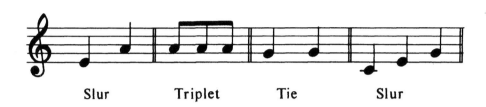

Slur   Triplet   Tie   Slur

6. GAME

FIND THE KEY

Write the correct music symbols in the boxes in column one then draw a line from each to the correct KEY SIGNATURE in column two in which you also must write the correct music symbols.

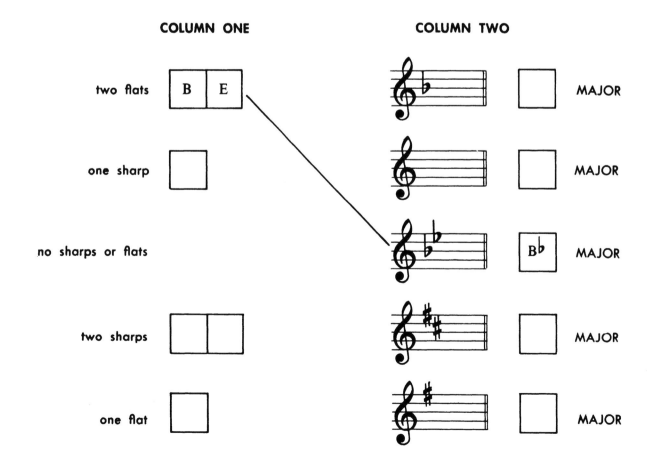

COLUMN ONE   COLUMN TWO

two flats   [B | E]

one sharp   [   ]

no sharps or flats

two sharps   [|]

one flat   [   ]

MAJOR

MAJOR

[B♭] MAJOR

MAJOR

MAJOR

BOOK TWO

LESSON EIGHT

Pupil's Name _____ Date _____ Grade (or Star) _____

1. READING

Read this poem aloud.

Fill in the missing letters to see
if you read the poem correctly.

WH _ N I S _ _ _ _ _ _ O _ ILS

_ _ R _ N _ N _ _ R,

I KNOW TH _ T SPRIN _ IS _ LMOST

H _ R _.

2. WRITING

Write these notes one octave
(8 notes) higher on the treble
staff.

Write these notes one octave
(8 notes) lower on the bass
staff.

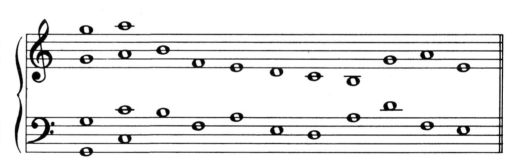

3. SPELLING

Spell the words that the notes
represent. Print them in the
boxes above and below the
notes.

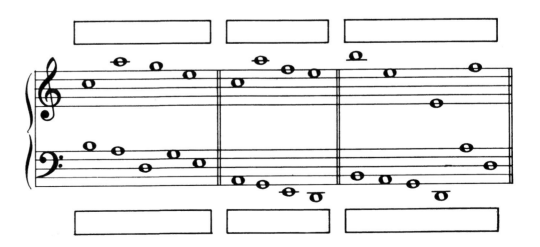

4. COUNTING

Add only ONE note or ONE rest to complete each measure for the correct time signature.

5. DRAWING

Here are some TIES and SLURS. In the TIED notes draw a cross on the note you would count and hold but not strike.

6. GAME
RIDDLES

Print the answer to each Riddle in the box.

Who is someone very small?

What can you ride in?

What do you check when you fly on an airplane?

What vegetable has a green head?

Where do you go at night?

Name a juicy steak.

What part of you do you see when you look in a mirror?

What does a sheriff wear?

Where is a good place to eat?

What does a chicken give you?

What do you do in arithmetic?

What do you carry groceries in?

BOOK TWO

LESSON NINE

Pupil's Name _____ Date _____ Grade (or Star) _____

1. READING

READ THIS ALOUD: A dot placed after a note adds ONE HALF of the value of the note to it.

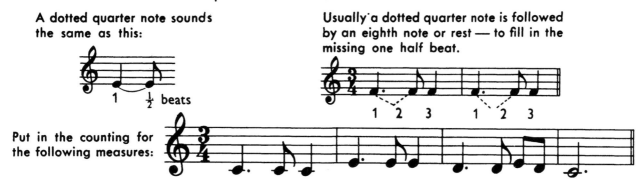

A dotted quarter note sounds the same as this:

1   ½ beats

Usually a dotted quarter note is followed by an eighth note or rest — to fill in the missing one half beat.

Put in the counting for the following measures:

2. WRITING

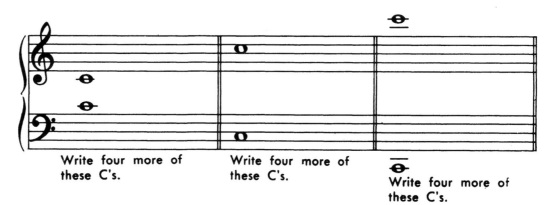

Write four more of these C's.

Write four more of these C's.

Write four more of these C's.

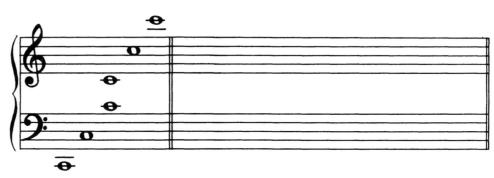

Write four more of these C's four more times:

3. COUNTING

Join the stems of some of these notes so there will be the correct number of beats in each measure.

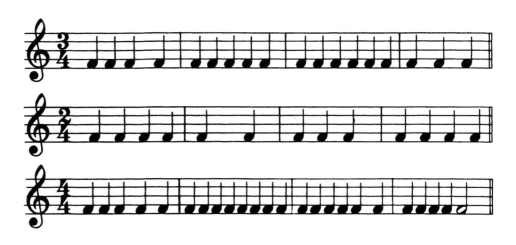

20

4. SPELLING

These notes spell words.
Print the words in the boxes
above and below the notes.

(The words in the treble clef
are different from the words
in the bass! So be careful!)

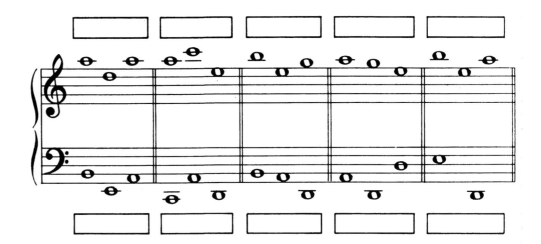

5. DRAWING

Draw a circle around
every C.

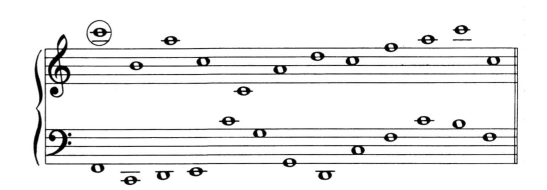

6. GAME

NAME TWO NAMES!

Draw a line to each of
the TWO NAMES for each
black key.

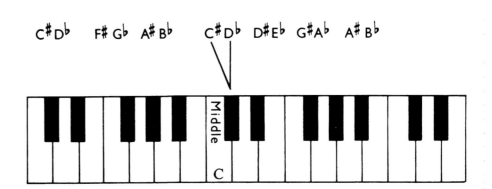

Draw a line from each note
to the black key it matches.

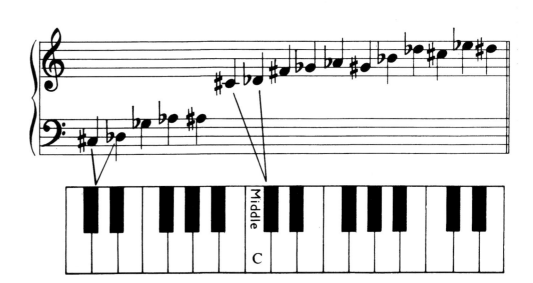

BOOK TWO

LESSON TEN

Pupil's Name _____ Date _____ Grade (or Star) _____

1. READING

READ THIS ALOUD!

The words Da Capo (Abbreviated, D. C.) mean to go back to the beginning.

The word Fine means THE END of the piece.

D. C. al Fine means to go back to the beginning and **play to the end of the piece.**

Here is a diagram of how to play D. C. al Fine.

The words DAL SEGNO (Abbreviated, D. S.) mean go back to this sign 𝄋

D. S. al Fine means to go back to this sign 𝄋 and play to the end of the piece.

Here is a diagram of how to play D. S. al Fine.

When you see a sign like this ⌐1⌐ :‖ ⌐2⌐ at the end of a piece, it means the piece has TWO ENDINGS.

The first time, play through the FIRST ENDING only — to the repeat sign — then go back to the beginning and play the piece again — but this time do NOT play the first ending when you come to it. SKIP IT AND PLAY THE SECOND ENDING.

Here is a diagram of how to play a FIRST and SECOND ENDING.

2. SPELLING

Spell correctly as you write the musical word or the abbreviation for it in the following:

gradually slower _____

smooth _____

short, detached _____

gradually louder _____

gradually softer _____

gradually faster _____

the end _____

W.M.Co., 9857

3. WRITING

Write three more notes with the same letter name above each of the notes in the bass clef.

Write the letter name of each set in the boxes below them.

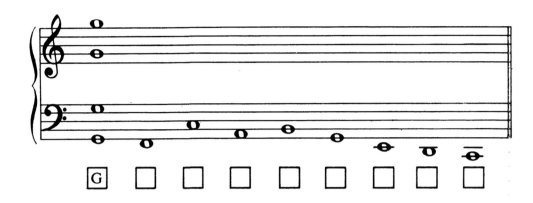

G								

4. COUNTING

Use notes or rests to complete these measures:

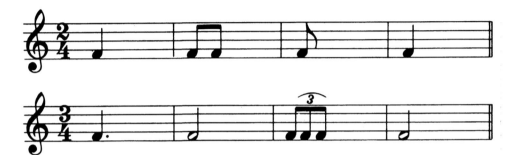

5. DRAWING

Draw a line from each diagram to its correct meaning:

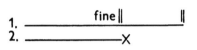

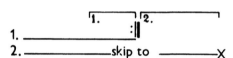

1. _____ fine ‖ ‖   D. S. al Fine.
2. _____X

1. _____ 𝄋 fine ‖ ‖   First and second endings.
   2. _____X

┌1.┐ ┌2.┐
1. _____ :‖   D. C. al Fine.
2. _____skip to _____X

6. GAME

CROSS WORD PUZZLE

Cue List

Down

1. gradually slower (Abbreviation).
2. gradually softer (Abbreviation).
3. smooth.
4. gradually louder (Abbreviation).
5. time.

Across

6. short, detached.
7. the end.
8. gradually faster (Abbreviation).

PUZZLE

BOOK TWO

LESSON ELEVEN

Pupil's Name _____ Date _____ Grade (or Star) _____

1. READING

READ THIS ALOUD!

This music does NOT begin on the first count. It begins with an INCOMPLETE MEASURE, so the last measure must balance with the first by having only the number of counts that were omitted in the first measure.

2. WRITING

Write notes with the same letter name one octave above in the treble clef and one octave below in the bass clef.

Write the names of the notes in the boxes.

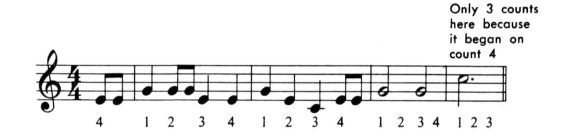

3. COUNTING

Put in time signatures and number the counts for each of the following:

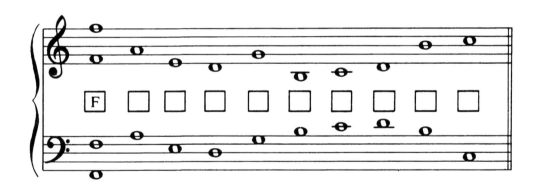

W.M.Co., 9857

4. SPELLING

Spell the words needed to complete this jingle.
Print the words in the boxes.

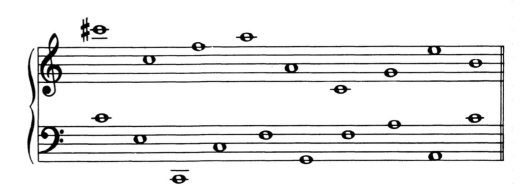

I like to [   ] ducks at the [   ] of the lake.

They [   ] to be [   ] as they flutter and shake.

5. DRAWING

Draw a sharp sign before every leger line note.

Draw a flat sign before every space note.

Draw a natural sign before every line note.

6. GAME

MYSTERY TUNE

This is the beginning of a well known tune.
Sing it to yourself (not playing the notes).
Write the name of the tune in the box above the music.

BOOK TWO

LESSON TWELVE

Pupil's Name _____ Date _____ Grade (or Star) _____

1. READING

As you read the notes, print their letter names in the boxes above and below them.

2. WRITING

Write the name of the KEY SIGNATURE in the box under each of the following:

☐ Major ☐ Major ☐ Major ☐ Major ☐ Major

3. COUNTING

Put in the time signature and number the counts in each of these three examples:

4. SPELLING

Spell correctly as you write the musical words for each of the following:

time _____

smoothly _____

moderate speed _____

quick and lively _____

slowly _____

the end _____

W.M.Co., 9857

5. DRAWING

Draw the musical sign for each word at the end of the arrows:

accent ⎯⎯⎯⎯⟶

repeat ⎯⎯⎯⎯⟶

tie ⎯⎯⎯⎯⟶

hold ⎯⎯⎯⎯⟶

staccato ⎯⎯⎯⟶

slur ⎯⎯⎯⎯⟶

triplet ⎯⎯⎯⟶

gradually louder ⎯⟶

gradually softer ⎯⟶

Draw a diagram showing how to play each of the following:

D. C. al FINE.

D. S. al FINE.

FIRST AND SECOND ENDINGS.

6. GAME

TWENTY QUESTIONS — TRUE OR FALSE

Print a "T" if it is true — or an "F" if it is false after each of the following:

1. Cresc. means time. ___
2. Dim. means gradually softer. ___
3. Accel. means gradually slower. ___
4. Rit. means gradually slower. ___
5. Tempo means time. ___
6. This sign ⌢ means repeat. ___
7. Fine means the end. ___
8. Legato means smooth. ___
9. This ♩♩ is a slur. ___
10. The key signature of F MAJOR has one flat — B. ___
11. D. S. al Fine means to go back to the beginning and play to "Fine". ___

12. This ♪ is an eighth note. ___
13. This 𝄾 is an eighth rest. ___
14. This is a triplet ♪♪♪ . ___
15. This sign ƒƒ means to play softly. ___
16. This sign ◁ means to play gradually louder. ___
17. This sign ▷ means to play gradually softer. ___
18. This ♩. is a dotted quarter note. ___
19. A whole measure rest always gets four beats. ___
20. F SHARP is the same as G flat on the keyboard. ___

W.M.Co.. 9857

A DOZEN A DAY

by Edna Mae Burnam

The **A Dozen A Day** books are universally recognized as one of the most remarkable technique series on the market for all ages! Each book in this series contains short warm-up exercises to be played at the beginning of each practice session, providing excellent day-to-day training for the student. The CD is playable on any CD player and features fabulous backing tracks by Ric Iannone. For Windows® and Mac users, the CD is enhanced so you can access MIDI files for each exercise and adjust the tempo.

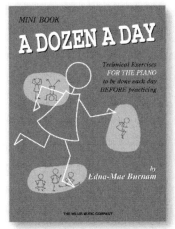
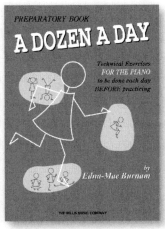
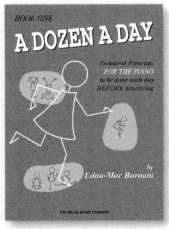
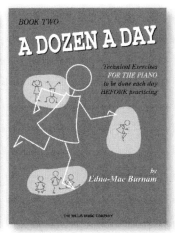

MINI BOOK
00404073 Book Only $4.99
00406472 Book/CD $9.99

PREPARATORY BOOK
00414222 Book Only $4.99
00406476 Book/CD $9.99

BOOK 1
00413366 Book Only $4.99
00406481 Book/CD $9.99

BOOK 2
00413826 Book Only $4.99
00406485 Book/CD $9.99

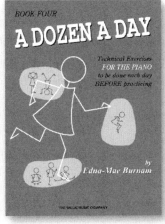
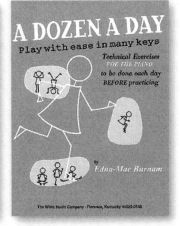

BOOK 3
00414136 Book Only $5.99
00416760 Book/CD $10.99

BOOK 4
00415686 Book Only $5.99
00416761 Book/CD $10.99

PLAY WITH EASE IN MANY KEYS
00416395 Book Only $4.99

WILLIS MUSIC

EXCLUSIVELY DISTRIBUTED BY

HAL•LEONARD®

Prices, contents, and availability subject to change without notice. Prices listed in U.S. funds.

A DOZEN A DAY SONGBOOK SERIES
BROADWAY, MOVIE AND POP HITS
Arranged by Carolyn Miller

The *A Dozen a Day Songbook* series contains wonderful Broadway, movie and pop hits that may be used as companion pieces to the memorable technique exercises in the *A Dozen a Day* series. They are also suitable as supplements for ANY method!

Mini
Early Elementary

A DOZEN A DAY
SONGBOOK

Broadway, Movie and Pop Hits
Any Dream Will Do • Can You Feel the Love Tonight • A Dream Is a Wish Your Heart Makes
Heigh-Ho • I'm Popeye the Sailor Man • It's a Grand Night for Singing • Lean on Me
Love Me Tender • So Long, Farewell • You'll Never Walk Alone

THE WILLIS MUSIC COMPANY

MINI
EARLY ELEMENTARY
Songs in the Mini Book:
Any Dream Will Do • Can You Feel the Love Tonight • A Dream Is a Wish Your Heart Makes • Heigh-Ho • I'm Popeye the Sailor Man • It's a Grand Night for Singing • Lean on Me • Love Me Tender • So Long, Farewell • You'll Never Walk Alone.

00416858 Book Only $6.99

00416861 Book/CD Pack.........$12.99

PREPARATORY
MID-ELEMENTARY
Songs in the Preparatory Book:
The Bare Necessities • Do-Re-Mi • Getting to Know You • Heart and Soul • Little April Shower • Part of Your World • The Surrey with the Fringe on Top • Swinging on a Star • The Way You Look Tonight • Yellow Submarine.

00416859 Book Only $6.99

00416862 Book/CD Pack.........$12.99

BOOK 1
LATER ELEMENTARY
Songs in Book 1:
Cabaret • Climb Ev'ry Mountain • Give a Little Whistle • If I Were a Rich Man • Let It Be • Rock Around the Clock • Twist and Shout • The Wonderful Thing About Tiggers • Yo Ho (A Pirate's Life for Me) • Zip-A-Dee-Doo-Dah.

00416860 Book Only $6.99

00416863 Book/CD Pack.........$12.99

BOOK 2
EARLY INTERMEDIATE
Songs in Book 2:
Hallelujah • I Dreamed A Dream • I Walk the Line • I Want to Hold Your Hand • In the Mood • Moon River • Once Upon A Dream • This Land is Your Land • A Whole New World • You Raise Me Up.

00119241 Book Only $6.99

00119242 Book/CD Pack.........$12.99

Prices, content, and availability subject to change without notice.

WILLIS MUSIC

EXCLUSIVELY DISTRIBUTED BY

HAL•LEONARD®

www.willispianomusic.com   **www.facebook.com/willispianomusic**

The Composer's Choice series showcases piano works by an exclusive group of composers, all of whom are also teachers and performers. Each collection contains classic piano pieces that were carefully chosen by the composer, as well as brand-new compositions written especially for the series. The composers also each contributed helpful and valuable performance notes for each collection. Get to know a new Willis composer today!

FROM WILLIS MUSIC

ELEMENTARY

COMPOSER'S CHOICE – GLENDA AUSTIN
8 Original Piano Solos
MID TO LATER ELEMENTARY LEVEL
Betcha-Can Boogie • Jivin' Around • The Plucky Penguin • Rolling Clouds • Shadow Tag • Southpaw Swing • Sunset Over the Sea • Tarantella (Spider at Midnight).
00130168 .... $6.99

COMPOSER'S CHOICE – CAROLYN MILLER
8 Original Piano Solos
MID TO LATER ELEMENTARY LEVEL
The Goldfish Pool • March of the Gnomes • More Fireflies • Morning Dew • Ping Pong • The Piper's Dance • Razz-a-ma-tazz • Rolling River.
00118951 .... $6.99

COMPOSER'S CHOICE – CAROLYN C. SETLIFF
8 Original Piano Solos
EARLY TO LATER ELEMENTARY LEVEL
Dark and Stormy Night • Dreamland • Fantastic Fingers • Peanut Brittle • Six Silly Geese • Snickerdoodle • Roses in Twilight • Seahorse Serenade.
00119289 .... $6.99

INTERMEDIATE

COMPOSER'S CHOICE – GLENDA AUSTIN
8 Original Piano Solos
EARLY TO MID-INTERMEDIATE LEVEL
Blue Mood Waltz • Chromatic Conversation • Etude in E Major • Midnight Caravan • Reverie • South Sea Lullaby • Tangorific • Valse Belle.
00115242 .... $8.99

COMPOSER'S CHOICE – ERIC BAUMGARTNER
8 Original Piano Solos
EARLY TO MID-INTERMEDIATE LEVEL
Aretta's Rhumba • Beale Street Boogie • The Cuckoo • Goblin Dance • Jackrabbit Ramble • Journey's End • New Orleans Nocturne • Scherzando.
00114465 .... $8.99

COMPOSER'S CHOICE – RANDALL HARTSELL
8 Original Piano Solos
EARLY TO MID-INTERMEDIATE LEVEL
Above the Clouds • Autumn Reverie • Raiders in the Night • River Dance • Showers at Daybreak • Sunbursts in the Rain • Sunset in Madrid • Tides of Tahiti.
00122211 .... $8.99

COMPOSER'S CHOICE – CAROLYN MILLER
8 Original Piano Solos
EARLY INTERMEDIATE LEVEL
Allison's Song • Little Waltz in E Minor • Reflections • Ripples in the Water • Arpeggio Waltz • Trumpet in the Night • Toccata Semplice • Rhapsody in A Minor.
00123897 .... $8.99